A
STRAIGHTFORWARD
GUIDE
TO
EFFECTIVE
NEGOTIATING

David Blanchard
Straightforward Publishing

Straightforward Publishing
38 Cromwell Road
London E17 9JN
WWW. Straightforwardco.Co.U.K
E mail Info @ Straightforwardco.Co.U.K

ISBN: 1899924 29 9

Printed by Bath Press, Wiltshire

Cover Design by Straightforward Graphics

A STRAIGHTFORWARD GUIDE TO EFFECTIVE NEGOTIATING
CONTENTS

INTRODUCTION

ACKNOWLEDGEMENTS

Thanks is given to all those who have assisted with the writing of this book during the last year. It has been a difficult process and the final text was completed after many hours of negotiations!

INTRODUCTION

This brief introduction to the process of negotiations was the result of myself being unable to find a satisfactory text that would serve as an introduction for the many students that I teach.

Quite often people hear the word negotiation and immediately envisage a smoky room with a group of people sitting round, each trying to get what they want out of a situation and to defeat the others.

Of course, negotiation is usually nothing of the sort. We negotiate in all sorts of situations, the family, business, employment and in many other areas. The important thing to remember is that the fundamental techniques underpinning negotiations are the same whatever the situation.

Clear objectives, a well worked out strategy, knowledge of the variables involved, patience, a knowledge of the other side and flexibility are key elements of any negotiation.

This book leads the reader through all of the essential areas of negotiation and it is hoped that the reader will gain a clear insight into the processes and emerge a more skilled negotiator.

1
NEGOTIATING IN CONTEXT

What is negotiation?

There seems to be a lot of mystique attached to the word negotiation. Indeed, many people are afraid of the connotations attached to the word. However, everyone negotiates in some aspect of their life. It is not something that only certain people do. Negotiation is, fundamentally, a communication skill and one that is underpinned by the process of persuasion. One party tries to persuade the other to accept their point of view or to reach a point where each side is satisfied with the outcome.

Negotiation is concerned with the relationship between two parties where the needs of both are largely in balance. There are many times when you will be persuaded to do something, such as buy a new car or to do something on behalf of your company.

Essentially:

The balance of need of either party effectively defines the process of negotiation.

To be an effective negotiator, it is essential that you learn something about the process of negotiation and the skills inherent within that process. The circumstances calling for negotiation are many, including selling, buying, contractual negotiations such as employment or other organizational matters. However, in a great number of situations you need to be in possession of certain skills in order to be able to influence the outcome in a way that suits you. That is what the rest of this brief introduction to negotiation will concentrate on. How to communicate and persuade others to adopt a position which is suitable to you.

Communication and persuasion

As we stated, many people are intrigued by the process of negotiation. However, what is it that makes the process of negotiation so complicated and why do people wish to acquire the necessary skills to be able to conduct this process effectively?

Often, there are many complex twists and turns to discussions and the outcomes of such discussions cannot be simple. There are so many different angles to certain discussions that to achieve a satisfactory outcome to all parties concerned is very difficult indeed.

Essentially, there is a competitive, or adversarial aspect to negotiations. Each person involved wishes to ensure that they obtain the best result for themselves. However, this particular aspect must be controlled, in successful negotiation, so that each party involved can feel that they have achieved. If this is not the case, then what we have is not negotiation but outright confrontation.

The skilled negotiator will understand that the outcome of discussions must be felt to be equitable by all, even if, in fact, a party is left without the result they desired. In short, there is a very subtle psychology underpinning negotiation. This has to be understood as a prerequisite to successful and effective negotiation.

There is a vital element underpinning the whole process of influencing others-that is the art of *communication*. It is absolutely necessary to ensure that what you are saying is crystal clear to the other side. If it is not, you will never succeed in negotiation.

Communication can be viewed in several lights, there is the process of everyday communication, which involves those we interact with on a regular basis, or there is communication in the field of business, which is where most, but by no means all, communication takes place. However, the following points must be borne in mind:

- If what you are saying is unclear to the other side then the process of negotiation will run into problems

- If you are not exact or precise in what you are saying then you will run into problems

- If you jargonize then the other side will not understand and you will create problems

Essentially, clarity is of the utmost importance. There are two sides to this. The first is that if people are unclear about what it is you are saying, what point you are trying to make, then you cannot hope to persuade them which is the next vital step in negotiating.

In addition, you yourself will lose the thread of what it is you are talking about, or what you are trying to achieve and will put yourself in a position where you will lose whatever ground you have gained.

Persuading others

It is very easy for communication to end up being unpersuasive. This very much depends on the approach taken toward the other person, and whether or not their point of view is taken into consideration. People will not be persuaded if they think that someone is 'trying to get one over on them'. Instead they will close up and be defensive and negotiations will go nowhere.

Generally, you have to start by thinking of the thought processes involved when considering another persons involvement. This process is one that is seen to move through a number of stages:

- The other persons need to feel important and respected

- Consideration of the others needs

- The need to feel that the proposition being put forward will be of benefit

- The need to understand the facts

- The need to understand the pitfalls

- The need to understand what to do

- The desire, or otherwise, to approve what is being put forward.

This is part of the weighing up process, assessing the good against the bad and attempting to come to a decision.

Any attempt at communication that results in an unsatisfactory response in any of the above stages is unlikely to end in agreement. This is because the process of "frustration" has occurred and there will be delays whilst problems are sorted out and points are clarified. Among the many techniques of persuasion in existence, matching the persons decision making thoughts and describing your own case in a way that reflects that, is key.

Successful outcomes do not always arise from the initial contact between those involved in the decision making process. Because of the complexity and the fact that there may be frustration in the process then other meetings may be necessary. It is essential to think ahead and try to see where you went wrong. Ensure that you are aware of the processes as described and that you can analyze each stage and prepare yourself for the next round.

If persuasion is to succeed, it is necessary to tackle communication with a clear eye on the listener and their point of view. The whole approach must be seen to be, and must come over as, acceptable. There are several factors that join to make a person's manner acceptable:

- Projection

- Empathy

Essentially, projection means the way we come over to other people. When people are in a position of stress they quite often project as a way of off loading on to other people. Empathy means the ability to understand another, to put yourself in their place and to understand how they feel and how you would feel if you were there. The other person must feel that you are empathizing with them.

It is worth, at this point, taking a look at the different types of communication, and communicators, each with varying degrees of empathy and thus success:

- There is the person who is very aggressive and oversensitive. They quite often win arguments but they project without empathy. This becomes self-defeating and will serve to close up others, who become very defensive.

- There is the person who has very little interest in the whole process and conveys that. This lack of commitment leads to a lack of conclusion

- There is the weak communicator. They come over nice and well meaning but do not achieve a lot. Basically, they will take the side of the other party to the negotiations and they achieve little

- The ideal communicator has a creative understanding of the listener and is often a sensitive person, being empathetic with others. As we stated, being seen to have understood the others point of view is essential to successful outcomes in negotiations.

Only when someone is persuaded in principle towards a particular course of action will they be interested in moving on to the stage of making a deal.

Now read the main points from chapter one.

MAIN POINTS FROM CHAPTER ONE

- Negotiation is primarily concerned with the relationships between two parties where the needs of both are largely in balance.

- The skilled negotiator will understand that the outcome of discussions must be felt to be equitable by all, even if, in fact, a party is left without the result that they desired.

- In negotiations, competitive adversarial instincts must be controlled and the position and the needs of others understood.

- Negotiation is, above all, a communication skill, one that is underpinned by the process of persuasion. Communication and persuasion are key concepts that must be understood by all negotiators.

2
THE PEOPLE FACTOR

In chapter one, we discussed the main elements underpinning negotiation. We defined negotiation and saw that the crucial elements in the process of negotiation are communication and persuasion. We will be exploring communication further in this chapter.

However, **negotiators are people first.** When negotiating, it is easy to forget that the "other side" are people too. People have emotions, deeply held beliefs and values, they often come from different backgrounds and have different opinions. They are as unpredictable as you are.

A working relationship where understanding, respect and trust have been built up can help the negotiation process enormously. Peoples desire to feel good about themselves, and their concern for what others will think about them, can often make them more sensitive to another negotiators interests.

On the other hand, people can be afraid and angry and also feel frustrated and hostile. They can misinterpret what you say. Misunderstanding can reinforce prejudice and rational negotiation can break down. The purpose of the game then becomes one of scoring points and apportioning blame.

Failing to deal with others sensitively and recognize that we are all prone to human reactions can be disastrous for negotiation. It is therefore essential that, whatever else you are doing at any point in the negotiation process, you ask yourself " am I paying enough attention to the people factor"?

It is useful to focus on the people factor by breaking it down into three categories:

- Perception

- Emotion

- Communication

Perception

Often the problem lies not only in objective reality but also in peoples heads. The difference between your thinking and theirs. Fears, even if ill founded are quite often real fears and need to be dealt with. Hopes, even if unrealistic, cause conflict. It is the reality as each side sees it that constitutes the problem in a negotiation, recognizing that this opens the way for a solution. Therefore:

- Put yourself in their shoes

- Don't deduce their intentions from your fears

- Avoid blaming them for your problem

- Make perceptions explicit and discuss them

- Look for opportunities to act consistently with another's perceptions

- Involve people in the process

- Face saving-make your proposals consistent with their values

Emotion

In a negotiation feelings may be more important than words. Parties may be more ready for battle than for co-operatively working out a solution to a common problem. People often come to a negotiation feeling that the stakes are high and feel threatened. Emotions on the one side generate emotions on the other. Fear may breed anger and anger fear. Emotions may quickly bring negotiation to a deadlock.

- Recognize and understand emotions, yours and theirs

- Make emotions explicit and acknowledge them as legitimate

- Allow the other side to let off steam

- Don't react emotionally to emotional outbursts

- Use symbolic gestures

Communication

As we have seen, without communication there is no negotiation. Negotiation is a process of communicating back and forth for the purpose of reaching a joint decision. Communication is never an easy thing, even for people who have an enormous background of shared values and experience. Where two people are in a situation where suspicion or hostility are common feelings, it is not surprising that communication is poor.

There are three main problems:

1. The negotiators may not be talking to each other, or at least not in a way to be understood.

2. Even if you are talking clearly and directly to them, they may not be hearing you.

3. Misunderstanding.

To overcome these problems we need to:

- Listen actively and acknowledge what is being said

- Speak to be understood

- Speak about yourself, not them

- Speak for a purpose.

Although these techniques for dealing with problems of perception, emotion and communication usually work well, the best time for handling the people factor is before they become problems. This means building a personal and organizational relationship with the other side, and structuring the negotiation in ways that separate the substantive problem from the relationship.

Now read the main points from chapter two

MAIN POINTS FROM CHAPTER TWO

- It must be clearly understood that negotiators are people first, with emotions, deeply held beliefs and values. People also have widely differing opinions. The skilled negotiator should therefore be a skilled psychologist and empathize with others.

- A working relationship where understanding, respect and trust have been built up will assist the negotiation process enormously. This requires awareness of the people factor: perception, emotion and communication.

3

NEGOTIATION TECHNIQUES

Having acknowledged the importance of communication and also examined the significance of the importance of people in the negotiation process, we need now to look at the basis of negotiation techniques.

The process of negotiation needs to be understood clearly. There is obviously more to negotiation than just sitting down and agreeing or disagreeing. Otherwise, books would not be written on the subject and people would not go on to expensive seminars. A question posed to me was "why do you need to write a book to help people make decisions"? My response was that the more complicated the subject matter and the greater the potential losses the harder it is for all parties to the process to come to an agreement.

Coming to an agreement can be seen in the light of what is known as "win-win" dealing. It is absolutely fundamental to the process of negotiation that both the parties involved end up feeling satisfied that a deal appropriate to their needs has been done and that the end result is reasonably acceptable to them. As we have discussed, each side must also feel that they have been understood by the other parties to the negotiations and there has not been an attempt to "rip them off".

Negotiation is not a process whereby one party feels that they must win at all costs.

This is not negotiation this is aggression and hostility and bullying the other side into submission. Negotiation is a process of give and take, flexibility and meeting somewhere outside of what was originally desired.

We need to look at some of the finer points of the processes underlying win-win negotiations:

- The approach should be one of seeking common ground, as opposed to trying to get your way on everything

- You need to show that you empathize with the other parties to the negotiations, rather than merely objecting to them

- Be ready to compromise

- Discussions within a negotiation framework must encompass debate that goes to and fro rather than being conducted within a rigid framework

- Discussions within a negotiating framework should consist of questioning-and listening-rather than mere statements of ones case

- Be open, disclosing appropriate information to the other side rather than being defensive and secretive

- The emphasis should be on building relationships with parties to a negotiation rather than instilling bad feelings

- The aim in all negotiations is that of agreement. Quite often the end result is one of stalemate because of lack of understanding and intransigence.

Identifying terms and conditions of negotiations

The key point when conducting negotiations is that the outset of negotiation is the process of identification of actual terms and conditions of whatever deal you are involved in. The arranging and agreement of terms and conditions then has to take place. Once this has taken place you can then move onto the actual discussions.

When you reach a crucial stage in negotiations, where a persons mind has been influenced and he or she has been persuaded of your case, and agreement in principle begins to emerge, it is time to begin to think "on what basis will the other party agree?"

At this point it is time to consider detail and for each party to decide whether all points of the deal suit them. Total satisfaction will probably not result but the balance must be right.

Variables in negotiation

Underlying all negotiations are the variables that must be considered. Variables are the basic raw materials of negotiation. There are often many variables and for certain when negotiating you need an idea of the nature and type and number of variables and also an idea of the importance. The more variables that there are, and the more difficult to rank, or prioritize, the more complex the negotiation becomes. In addition, human interactions inherently complicate the negotiation.

Having considered the variables and ranked them in order of importance, then it is time to consider what exactly brings success in the process of negotiation. Success rests on three factors:

- What you do

- How you go about it

- Preparation

The first two elements are wholly dependent on preparation. Sound preparation can give you the all-important "edge" which gives you a head start in comparison with the next person.

Preparation for negotiation

Being well prepared breeds confidence. Appearing confident will be seen by others as competence. Preparation itself may be just a few moments thought prior to negotiation, or it may mean a few hours with colleagues.

Whatever, it is of vital importance if you wish to maintain an edge. When preparing:

- Consider others involved in the process

- Consider your own position in relation to others

Consider what type of negotiations you are preparing for:

- Win/win or lose/lose

- Bilateral or multilateral?

- Must agreement be reached?

- Will the agreement be enforceable?

- Will the other person be involved in the agreements implementation?

- Where and how will the negotiations be held?

List all the issues

- What are the main issues?

- Are there wider issues involved?

- How do the issues interrelate?

- What are the interests behind the issues?

- What exactly do you want?

Gather information about the subject-about the other persons position/interests.

Consider what information you need to offer during the negotiation and what you might expect in exchange.

Review past negotiations with the other person.

- What lessons can be learnt?

Consider your position if the negotiation fails

- What action will you take?

Assess the relative strengths and weaknesses of your position

- How much do you need the other person's co-operation and vice versa?

- What are your alternatives and what are the other persons?

- Whose side is time on? What deadlines do you both have?

With regard to all the issues at stake, decide on your:

- Opening offer demand

- Realistic optimum target

- Satisfaction level

- Walk away point or bottom line.

Decide what concessions you are prepared to make

- Consider the cost to you and value to the other person

- What order you will offer them in

Determine what your strongest arguments are in making your case

Decide on your strategy and tactics for conducting the negotiation. What attitude will you adopt? Friendly, co-operative, informal, formal rigid etc. Take account of the circumstances, the other person and your own personality.

- How much time have you got?

- How much authority do you have, want to have, don't have?

- If you are negotiating as a team, what role is each member taking?

Put yourself in the other person shoes

- What are his needs?

- What does he want?

- Review the entire checklist through his/her eyes.

Make an agenda for the meeting, including time and place

- Discuss it with the other person and be prepared to be flexible.

Rehearse if time and importance justify

Be prepared to be flexible during the negotiation, departing if necessary from the prepared position.

Other people

Negotiations take place with all sorts of people. They may or may not be known to you personally. You need to ask certain fundamental questions:

- What role or intentions does the other have?

- What needs do they have?

- What problems will they raise during the course of negotiations?

- What, if any, objections will they raise?

- Do they have the authority to decide things or must they defer to others?

Each specific situation will raise different issues, but the principle of thinking through how people may handle something is similar in each case. Do not overlook this, or assume familiarity makes it unnecessary. Even with people you know and deal with regularly, such analysis may pay dividends.

How you are seen in negotiations

The other party in negotiations is yourself and how you are perceived by others is very important. If you appear professional and competent you will gain respect. If you appear flustered and convey the impression that you do not have control of the situation then you will very quickly lose respect. Underpinning the way you appear to others is confidence and this can only really be gained if you are prepared.

Setting Objectives in negotiations

It is essential that you have objectives set out very clearly in your own mind. You need to identify and set specific objectives, which can be measured. You need to have a clear set of priorities and they need to be very clearly linked to the variables involved. You need to understand your attitude to the variables and how far you may wish to compromise around each.

Timing of negotiations

It is very important to consider timing. For example, are you intent on achieving everything at once or are you prepared to wait until a satisfactory outcome is achieved? If you have a clear set of objectives, and understand the variables involved, then you can begin to get a clear idea of the time frame within which you want to achieve your goals.

The structure of a meeting

Structure means the actual shape and style, thus form, of the meeting. Structure includes everything that helps the meeting along and avoids muddles. Account needs to be taken of likely timing of the meeting. Your order of sequence and priority must fit within the duration of the meeting. You will need to be very clear about priorities and which are primary matters in negotiation, i.e., matters of the most importance and also secondary matters.

Remember, preparation is of vital importance and without effective groundwork you may lose that all important edge and thus not gain what you want.

Now read the main points from chapter three overleaf.

MAIN POINTS FROM CHAPTER 3

- The more complicated the subject matter, the greater the potential losses, the harder it is for all parties to come to an agreement.

- Coming to an agreement can be seen in the light of what is known as 'win-win' dealing. It is fundamental to the process of negotiation that both parties involved end up feeling satisfied that a deal appropriate to their needs has been concluded, and that the end result is reasonably acceptable to them.

- The approach, overall, should be that of seeking common ground. Be ready to compromise and accept debate.

- Make sure that you recognise all the variables in your negotiations. You must rank, or prioritise, these variables.

- Ensure that you are well prepared. This breeds confidence. Be aware of all the issues and decide beforehand what concessions you are prepared to make. Be prepared to be flexible.

- When planning negotiations, set out clear attainable objectives.

4
PREPARING FOR NEGOTIATIONS

Negotiations are generally quite complicated and it is essential that meetings are managed effectively. Negotiations involve two separate processes that interact together:

- Tactics of negotiators

- The behavior of each of the negotiators

Tactics

Occasionally, the balance of power is very definitely slanted in one party's favor. In this case the result is often in no doubt. However, in most situations that involve negotiation, the balance of power is dispersed and certain acts are required to swing the balance. Both sides bring the power to negotiate to the table. Power can mean the following:

Specific variables

The most obvious sources of power are the specific variables that are most important to a negotiation. These can be anything, from finance to commodities. Variables can be both tangible and intangible and usually both are involved.

Reward

This is something that you can offer to the other party if they can be influenced. If you have something that the other wants then they will listen.

Threats of punishment

This is where there is an apparent intention not to give something that the other side wants.

Legitimacy

Legitimacy means the factual evidence. It can swing the balance without much argument. For example, this can be a written quote from another party which may prove that the point you are making to the demands being made are legitimate based on the evidence of someone else's perception of price.

Confidence

Confidence in negotiations will almost certainly arise from initial preparation. It is hard to deal with someone who appears to be very confident and you wish to ensure that the confident person is you.

The key principles of negotiation

There are four guiding principles that combine to help the process of negotiation. These are as follows:

- Set your sights as high as possible

- Find out the other persons intentions

- Keep the entirety of the factors in play in mind

- Keep looking for further variables

Setting sights high

Always aim high. You can always work your way downwards from the highest point if you want. However, it is difficult to trade up.

Finding out the other persons full intentions

The more complete the picture of the other person the better. The more that you know about their requirements the easier it is to decide exactly what you are going to give, or otherwise. You need as much information about the other person as possible and quite often this comes from prior preparation.

Keeping all factors in mind

As the picture builds up so the process becomes more complex. It is easy as you plan ahead to forget some of the issues that you need to keep in mind. You need to have a clear head, make notes and to plan ahead as you go.

Keeping a look out for further variables

You need to remain flexible at all times. Avoid getting locked into previous plans. The good negotiator is quick on their feet.

Sometimes, what happens is very much along the lines that you expected. However, some fine-tuning is always necessary.

The process of negotiation assumes a balance. Although participants are often initially far apart on the scale and there is a perceived imbalance, both parties will settle on something that is assumed reasonable. This is why people accept. In very few instances do parties walk away from the negotiating table feeling aggrieved.

The initial stance of parties

The initial stance refers to the starting point that each party begins with. There are a number of options:

Going for the quick kill

This is the extreme end of the scale where one party says to another "take it or leave it" This is a very hard approach and is difficult to deal with although does not rule out negotiations. Anyone starting from this point obviously thinks that they are in a position of power to begin with.

Taking a more flexible approach

At the other end of the scale the conversation might begin on a more flexible note, such as "lets talk about what you want and see if we can't arrive at a compromise". This is more suitable when the negotiators do not have a particularly strong case and wish to arrive at a reasonable solution.

It is said that the higher the opening stance the better the final deal achieved. It is difficult to negotiate down from nothing and an initially extreme stance can throw the other off balance. Ultimately, the first phase of negotiations is only a clarification of initial stances. Soon after, a less extreme point is adopted by each in the process that allows for negotiations proper to begin.

Bridge building

There is certainly a need to develop a rapport as the process proceeds. This brings the parties closer together and enables the other parties to the process to see your point of view. There are a number of key approaches to bridge building:

- Open the discussions on a neutral subject

- Show respect for the other party and the process of negotiations

- Refer back, if necessary, to past agreements. This helps reinforce persuasion.

- Be clear about complicated and complex issues

The above tactics during negotiations put the process on the basis of reason and flexibility rather than the proverbial brick wall. Adopting these tactics results in bridges being constructed throughout the process.

It is important to ask questions of the other parties to the process and really be clear as to their intentions and what they mean. It is at this stage that you may wish to begin trading concessions. You should avoid giving anything away early on in the process. This is very important indeed.

Never give a concession. Appear to be trading it reluctantly. You want to be seen by the other parties as driving a hard bargain. If you don't then you will not be taken seriously. It is important, in this context to optimize your concessions and minimize the other parties. Optimizing your concessions means:

- Stressing the cost to you

- Exaggerating, but maintaining a certain credibility

- Refer to a major problem that a concession made by you will solve

- Imply that you are making a major concession.

Minimizing concessions

This means:

- Do not overdo thanks. Don't be too profuse

- Depreciating them, minimizing the value

- Treating them as having very little value

- Taking them for granted

- Devaluing them by implying that you already have what's on offer anyway

- Denying any value

Concessions are either minimized or optimized as deemed appropriate. The skilled negotiator will trade a concession which in fact will cost them little. It has, though, an implied value which brings a relatively more valuable concession in return from the other side. It is this difference in value that gives an edge.

The use of techniques

There are other techniques that are very important in negotiation. These are:

Use of silence

Keeping quiet can be as powerful as speaking. Silence can unnerve the other side and lead them to say something or give something away. It is difficult to maintain complete silence but inevitably something will give.

Summarizing frequently

Negotiations can sometime be very complicated. They often involve the juggling of a number of variables. It is very easy to lose direction. Never be afraid to recap on the process or to summarize in order to regain your thoughts.

Note taking

This also will help keep complex negotiations on track. Never put yourself in a position where you have to grope to remember what was said. This may call into question your level of expertise.

Taking notes will act as an aide memoir and ensure that you have all the facts at your fingertips.

You should remember that negotiation involves adversaries. Both parties want the best and both will try to get the best. Maintain neutrality as much as possible. Concentrate and keep ahead of the process. Be in charge of yourself and the process as a whole. Run the conversation in a way that you want and not a way that the other wants. Get off to a good start and remain conscious of what the other party wants and is trying to achieve.

Negotiation-further useful tips

Strategy

- Concentrate on persuading the other party rather than allow the negotiation to become a debate

- Don't confuse style and content. You can be a tough negotiator without being unpleasant or hostile.

- Differentiate between people and problems, make points rather than enemies.

- Don't allow fear of deadlock to influence your approach.

- Don't negotiate to a formula. Every situation will be different.

- Put yourself in the other person shoes.

- Recognize that successful negotiation is as much about avoiding bad agreements as making good agreements.

- Don't assume that your weaknesses are known to the other party

- Don't take the view that negotiation is primarily about splitting the difference.

- Leave the difficult issues until later in the negotiation.

Preparation

- Prepare thoroughly and systematically.

- Always enter negotiations with clear-cut targets and bottom lines.

- Make sufficient time for negotiation.

- Consider whether the negotiation might set precedents.

- Negotiation can be physically demanding-make sure that you have the stamina.

- Establish whether the other person has the authority to make the agreement.

- Make sure that you have sufficient information and use the negotiation itself to check existing information and acquire new information.

- In assessing relative strengths and weaknesses recognize that perceptions can be more important than reality.

Tactics

- Beware of starting to view your bottom line as your target.

- Be patient.

- Don't be too eager to please and so give in continually.

- Delay reaction until a proposal has been spelt out in full.

- Be aware that there are many more reactions to a proposal than acceptance or rejection. Try questioning the proposal, postponing reaction, comparing it to another proposal, and modifying it.

- Don't take every deadline too seriously.

- Don't offer concessions too easily or too early.

- Concessions made as part of your opening position will be take for granted.

- Be clear that you expect something in return for making a concession.

- Don't necessarily accept the first offer-first offers are rarely final offers.

- During negotiation make use of breaks for private discussions when negotiating as a team.

- Refrain from answering questions that you do not understand.

- Question whether an ultimatum is really serious.

- Don't be overly influenced by another persons opening position.

- Don't be nervous of making the first move.

- Listen and hear what the other person is saying.

- Avoid short-term negotiation tactics within the context of long term business relationships.

Now read the main points from chapter Four

MAIN POINTS FROM CHAPTER FOUR

- It is essential that meetings are managed effectively. Negotiations involve two separate processes that must be managed, tactics and behaviour.

- When negotiating, set your sites as high as possible, try to find out the other person's intentions.

- It is important to develop a rapport as the process proceeds. Be clear about complicated and complex issues.

- You should minimise concessions and optimise concessions as appropriate to the negotiation in question.

5

REACHING AGREEMENT

Having established the framework for negotiations and prepared yourself thoroughly it is necessary to consider the art of reaching an agreement and having all sides clearly recognizing the agreement and, most importantly, sticking by it.

It is important to bear in mind that some negotiations are informal and require no record of agreement. However, other negotiations are formal and it is essential that the agreement reached is documented and understood by all parties to the process.

Agreements in negotiations are usually contractual. Verbal agreements are contracts. Written agreements are binding. Therefore, it is essential that:

- Contractual situations are communicated clearly and reinforced if necessary, with no possibility of misunderstanding

- The contract enhances the relationship involved, if necessary on a continuing basis

- The contract allows the progressing and securing of agreement to proceed effectively and promptly.

Contractual arrangements need to make clear:

- The basis of the agreement

- The terminology to be used by both parties

- All elements of timing

- The procedures, documentation and administration involved

- All financial matters in detail

A contract may cause problems if it also causes surprises. Producing a hefty document for signature when there was no mention of it in the first place can cause upset. You need to make matters such as the outcome leading to a binding contract very clear from the outset.

The introduction of a contract, or the fact that there will be a contract has to be handled in the right way. Right at the outset you need to introduce the concept of a contract. You need to ensure that the details are crystal clear. Ensure that any figures and timing in the contract are clear to all parties. Check and double check the understanding. Document carefully your side of the arrangements and ask for their confirmation that they have understood.

If you deal with contractual matters in the right way then there should be minimal problems. However, what if the other party fails to comply with the contract? There are a number of options:

- Stick to the exact wording of the contract, also insisting that the other side do so

- Negotiate a compromise

- Make exceptions

Whatever you do, it is important not to allow the other party to deviate from the contract without recognition on your part.

It can be seen that communication is once again at the heart of reaching an agreement, ensuring that all involved clearly understand the agreement and that there are no problems once contracts are signed. However, it is vital that you receive others confirmation that all is understood and that they intend to abide by the agreement thereafter.

Now read the main points from Chapter five overleaf

MAIN POINTS FROM CHAPTER FIVE

- Depending on the type and form of negotiation, it is essential that agreements are formal, documented and finalised.

- Contractual arrangements need to make clear the basis of the agreement, the terminology to be used by all parties and elements of time, procedures and financial details in depth.

6

SECURING
IMPLEMENTATION

Reaching and documenting an agreement is not an end in itself. The purpose of any negotiation is to produce an outcome or action. In simple negotiations, the agreement and outcome might coincide. Seller and buyer bargain about a price, and immediately agreement is reached, the sale is concluded. In many cases, however, there is a delay between the close of negotiations and the agreed action's taking place. There may be an agreement too, on what the outcome may be, but no definition as to who has to do what in order to achieve this.

During the period of delay between agreement and action, or because of lack of clarity about implementation, some agreements fail to achieve their intended results. Attention to implementation is therefore crucial if effective negotiation is to be translated into effective action.

Three elements in the process require particular attention:

• including an implementation programme in the agreement

• establishing a joint implementation team

- ensuring adequate information and explanation to those affected by the agreement but not involved in the negotiations.

An agreed implementation programme

In any instance in which implementation of what has been agreed is not either or wholly unambiguous, the last part of the negotiation itself should be devoted to agreeing what has to be done, and by whom, to ensure the agreement is effected.

The same principle applies to even informal managerial discussions. To often, an agreement to do something is left hanging in mid-air without any definition of time scales or action plans. Three questions need to be answered about any agreement in which implementation is not coincident or immediate:

- When is action to implement going to be started?

- What has to be done to achieve implementation?

- Who is to undertake this work?

Joint implementation

In many cases, action should be taken by both parties to an agreement. For example, in the case of a new working hours agreement, management should brief the supervisors, and the union negotiators should brief the shop stewards. To ensure that both groups are given the same information, it may, therefore, be helpful to form a joint implementation team.

Joint implementation teams are common in a number of negotiation situations, for example, major business development programmes in which, after initial negotiations about fees or financial contributions, the parties involved evolve a partnership approach to the management of the agreed project.

Information and explanation

Most industrial relations agreements depend for their success on the actions of possibly thousands of individual managers, supervisors and trade union representatives-non of whom took part in the actual negotiations. Explaining such agreements fully and clearly to all concerned in their implementation is essential. Even in a small company, a deal struck between the chairman and the local union representative's needs to be explained to the supervisors and staff.

It is in this phase that imprecise wording in the original agreement can be very damaging. A phrase such as 'The company will take such reasonable steps as are practicable to reduce the risk of vehicle accidents within its premises' will be interpreted in widely different ways by different people-a potent source of dispute as to whether or not the agreement is being honoured.

Too often, information about agreements is limited to the issue of badly drafted notices, or to word-of-mouth messages that will become progressively distorted as they pass down the management chain. Any agreement of substance or complexity that concerns people not involved in the original negotiations merits a carefully designed and executed programme of information and explanation.

Another common fault in the industrial relations field, for example, is for each side to independently issue its own explanation-and for these explanations to differ. Joint agreement on explanatory information, or the issue of such information on a joint basis, is highly desirable.

Several questions should be asked:

- Who needs to know about this agreement if it is to be implemented effectively?

- What do they need to know?

- How is this information best communicated?

- By whom?

- Within what time-scales?

Now read the main points from chapter six

MAIN POINTS FROM CHAPTER SIX

- An agreement is not successful until it has been effectively implemented.

- It is often helpful to include an implementation programme as an integral part of a negotiated agreement.

- An implementation programme defines what has to be done, when, and by whom.

- For some agreements, implementation may be best effected by a joint team.

- Those affected by, or required to apply, an agreement need adequate information and explanation.

- Such action should be based on defining who needs to know what, how, and by whom this information should be given, by what methods, and to what time-scales.

7

HANDLING BREAKDOWN

It is a fact that negotiations are not always successful. It is necessary to give some thought to what action might be needed if agreement cannot be achieved. This kind of contingency planning accepts the uncertainties of the bargaining process and ensures that thought is given to the consequences of breakdown before, rather than after, the event.

Reviewing what would happen if the negotiation is unsuccessful may also influence the bargaining tactics and objectives. It may be realised, for example, that, in the event of breakdown, the other party could possibly take legal action and that one's own position at law is fairly weak.

In such circumstances, it would be unwise to set too high a target. The course of action very much depends on the nature and type of the negotiation.

The questions to be asked before negotiations begin are therefore:

- Can the matter be resolved by taking unilateral action?

- Is it feasible to maintain the status quo as an alternative to what was being pursued in the negotiation?

- Has the other party the power to inflict damage?

- Can the other side unilaterally refer the matter to a third party, such as the courts or an arbitrator?

- Should arbitration or legal action be considered as an option for one's own side?

- If referred to a third party, is the outcome likely to be less favourable to one's bottom limit?

- Might third party assistance in the form of conciliation or mediation be helpful?

The main options are to take unilateral action or to use third-party intervention-which can be of two kinds: conciliation (or mediation) and arbitration.

Unilateral action

One general rule underpinning negotiation is that negotiation is not necessary if the outcome can be achieved by direct action. However, like most rules, this one has exceptions. For example, in industrial relations there may be many circumstances in which an employer has the power to impose changes in working conditions, but on which it is normal to seek the agreement of trade unions. An agreed solution is much more likely to be implemented effectively than one that, by its imposition, alienates employees. There are parallel situations in many informal managerial interactions.

In most instances of this kind, however, the option of exercising ultimate power of authority is one that should be retained.

Whether or not to use it has to be a matter of judgement in the particular circumstances. Points to consider are:

- What will be the effect of imposition on the quality of the relationship with the other party?

- Has the other party the power and the will to be obstructive, even if not wholly able to prevent implementation of the proposed solution?

- Will any damage caused by a reaction to imposition be worse than either dropping the matter and retaining the status quo, or a reference to third party intervention.

Third party intervention

An analysis to the realities of breakdown may indicate that it would be unwise to proceed unilaterally, or that one has no power to do so. It may also be unacceptable or impossible for the postion that existed before the negotiation to continue. In such circumstances, third party intervention may be a useful option to consider. There are two main forms of third party involvement, though each has two variants.

Conciliation or mediation

In these forms, the third party does not produce a binding decision but works with the parties in dispute to help them reach agreement.

The conciliator ensures that the two parties are not misunderstanding each other, and that they have considered all possible angles. The emphasis is on helping them evolve their own agreed solution, not on the production of solutions by the conciliator. The mediator is expected to go further and, after listening to the two sides, to suggest solutions. Neither party, however, is under a formal obligation to accept the mediator's proposals.

Arbitration or court rulings

Here, the third party (arbitrator or a court or tribunal) considers the arguments of both parties and then produces a binding solution or ruling.

Whether arbitration is an option will depend on whether prior and joint agreement exists about its use. Without such agreement it is not normally open for one party to impose the use of an arbitrator on another. Ideally, both parties agree, before negotiations begin, that if they fail to reach agreement the matter will be referred to arbitration and each will abide by the arbitrator's decision.

The position is different where use of the legal system is concerned. Here, it is open for one party to pursue a legal claim whether or not the other wishes the matter to be dealt with in this way. The courts can, of course, be used only to resolve issues lying within the purview of statute or common law, and the most frequent use of the law is to deal with contractual disputes and with claims for damages or compensation.

Different types of conciliation and arbitration exist in different types of negotiation. Conciliation comes closest to normal negotiation and carries the least risk of matters being taken out of one's control. It does not, however, put the other side under heavy pressure to compromise and may not, therefore, be enough to shift the other party from a heavily entrenched position.

Mediation places the parties under much stronger psychological pressure-if short of enforcement-to accept a solution that may be significantly worse than the bottom line.

In arbitration, both parties give up control of the outcome, The risk therefore exists of having a position imposed that hitherto has been considered unacceptable. A very thorough and realistic assessment of the validity of one's own position and arguments is therefore essential before either agreeing to arbitration or allowing negotiations to reach an impasse from which enforceable arbitration or legal action is the only course open to the other side. A common failing is to be overoptimistic about the validity or the strength of one's own case, or to underestimate the other sides position. Assessing the weak points of one's own case is of almost more importance than recognising its strengths.

Now read the main points from chapter seven.

MAIN POINTS FROM CHAPTER SEVEN

- Giving Thought to the situation that would occur if the negotiations failed to achieve agreement is an essential part of planning for negotiation.

- It is unwise to allow a negotiation to fail if the probable outcome is worse than the position reached when breakdown occurs.

- The main options in handling breakdown are to take unilateral action to enforce an outcome or to seek third-party intervention.

- In considering unilateral action, thought should be given to the effect of such action on future working relationships.

- The least extreme form of third party assistance is conciliation, in which a conciliator works with the parties to help them reach agreement.

- A more direct form is mediation, in which both parties agree to consider (but are not bound to accept) a solution accepted by the mediator.

- The most powerful and risky form of third party resolution is arbitration-where both parties bind themselves in advance to accept the arbitrator's solution-or legal action through the courts and tribunals.

- Making sound decisions about the use of conciliation, mediation, or arbitration depends on thorough and accurate assessments of the strength of each party's case.

8

NEGOTIATION THROUGH WRITTEN AND TELEPHONE COMMUNICATION

In the next few chapters, we shall consider alternative forms of negotiation and also the role and use of the media in negotiations. So far, we have considered the important points of face to face negotiation and also what happens if negotiations break down.

There are, however, occasions when negotiation takes place over a telephone or through the written word. Although we think of negotiation as a face to face process, the process of written communication and also telephone conversations play an important part in negotiations, particularly in the preliminary stages of setting the scene for negotiations.

Negotiation by letter

It is quite often the case, particularly with commercial and industrial relations negotiations, that they begin by letter, or an exchange of letters. Although these letters may be a request for a meeting, time and place and so on, they are also used, in a number of cases, as a statement of an opening position or to set the tone for forthcoming negotiations. Letters should be considered as an essential part of the negotiation process and not just as an initial formality. Solicitors have long recognised this point, as their initial letters in certain cases are designed to jolt the recipients out of their complacency and to take the matter seriously.

Although, in some cases, it would be unwise to attempt to conduct negotiations solely by letter, there are some situations where such a course may offer advantages over face to face meetings:

- Time can be saved. Negotiation meetings can be time consuming and a brief exchange of letters can achieve results a lot quicker.

- It may be possible to avoid an otherwise emotional meeting and deal with the problem more rationally. It can also have the advantage of cutting certain people out of a meeting, those people being known for their belligerent or bellicose attitudes.

- The negotiation will be on record-an important point if there is the possibility of eventual legal action.

- If very complex proposals are involved, it is much easier to put these in writing, avoiding potential misunderstanding which can arise out of heated meetings.

In practice, a mixture of written and oral communications is the best procedure and is the usual way to conduct negotiations. Negotiations may commence with a short exchange of letters in which both parties outline their intentions. A meeting will then take place, a short adjournment will take place while proposals are considered and then agreement will be reached.

Negotiating by telephone

Long or complex negotiations cannot be carried out by phone. However, there are some cases where this method of negotiation can be very effective. The telephone can have an advantage whereby some people, at least, can be more co-operative than in a face to face meeting. The unplanned or unexpected nature of a phone call sometimes reduces the care and resistance usually exercised in face-to-face negotiations.

There is a danger, of course, that such attempts at quick deals over the phone will go wrong. Negotiators who try to get quick results by using the telephone should be reasonably confident that there opposite numbers have less skill in this particular type of bargaining.

Now read the main points overleaf

MAIN POINTS FROM CHAPTER EIGHT

- Face to face discussions are not the only form of negotiations-effective use can be made of correspondence and the telephone.

- An open letter can help set out the initial stances and styles of later negotiations.

- Dealing with all or part of a negotiation by correspondence can save valuable time, avoid emotional confrontation and enable carefully drafted proposals to be produced.

- Some negotiators are less resistant to proposals when discussing them on the telephone.

- Telephone negotiations may be used to settle minor or simple negotiating points very quickly.

9
HANDLING THE MEDIA

The media in general, newspapers, radio and television always focus in on major industrial relations issues, in particular when negotiations break down. The same interest is usually shown in highly publicised commercial battles. In recent years there have been two related developments that have brought managers into contact with the media, as opposed to just the heads of major national or international companies:

- A growth in local media has resulted in even quite local small scale negotiations being covered by news stories.

- To an increasing extent, companies are actively using the media-whether through advertisements or interviews-as a channel of communication to influence the outcome of commercial and industrial relations negotiations. Instead of just responding, often reluctantly, to media requests to statements, they are commissioning public relations and advertising consultants to advise on how the media can be used to promote their negotiating objectives, or to gain public understanding and support.

Negotiations cannot be conducted through the media, but in some situations thought should be given to the active use of the media as a channel of communication of influence, and to the response given to media requests for news and comments about negotiating issues of public interest.

If a manager becomes involved in media comment, or if it is decided to issue statements or notices to the media, the two main aspects to consider are:

- The characteristics of effective media communication.

- The choice of media and the method of communication.

Effective media communication

In any use of the media, two audiences are involved-the other party to the negotiation and the dispute, and the public at large. Public opinions can have a significant effect, particularly on employees during a strike. A feeling that public support has been lost can undermine striker's morale-and the opposite is also true. So one aim of media messages is to influence public attitudes.

In doing this, it must be remembered that whereas the public may not be able to spot errors or distortions in a story, those directly involved will, and this may well generate an even firmer resolve by the other party to continue their resistance.

There are, then, three main characteristics of effective media communications:

- Accuracy

- Clarity

- Reasonableness

There are a number of ways of getting a case into the public domain:

- press advertisements

- press releases

- press conferences

- news stories

- radio or TV interviews.

Press advertisements

There is only one way to retain local control over the wording and presentation of a message and avoid any editorial cutting-to buy advertising space. It is a method that has been used by large employers during industrial disputes, by major companies involved in takeover battles and by others.

If total control is the advantage, then the disadvantage is that the advertisement carries less weight with the public than news stories and editorial comment. Advertisements are taken with a pinch of salt and are seen as biased. There most effective use is probably to give very straightforward information, rather than views or comments.

Press releases

A press release is a prepared statement issued to the media for them to use as they think fit. As with the advertisement, it has the merit of being a statement that is, initially at least, under the control of the initiator. However, the resemblance ends there. The media have no obligation to print the statement as it stands, or at all. It may be ignored, because it is considered unnewsworthy. It may be reproduced in full. However, often it will be used as the basis for a news story written by journalists who may quote selectively from it

To stand the best chance of being used with minimum editorial interference, press releases should be clear and concise, written in the same style as the media use in their own stories.

Press conferences

On an issue for which maximum publicity is sought-perhaps to generate public opposition to a local authority's planning decision which has been the subject of abortive negotiation-the issue of a press release or official statement can be combined with a press conference. Media journalists are invited to attend, with the lure of a promise of a newsworthy statement followed by a question and answer session.

The advantage of a press conference is that it provides an opportunity to provide much more information and explanation than can be given in a short press release. There are three possible disadvantages or risks:

• No one may attend as a result of other more immediate news items taking priority that day.

• The questioning may be hostile, or concentrate on issues not central to the case that the company wants to make.

- No control can be exercised over the news stories that may be written.

News stories

A less formal, and often more successful, way of getting the organisation's case into the media is to telephone the relevant news desk, state that there is a story to tell, and invite a journalist to listen-either on the phone or at a meeting. Any resultant story is likely to be written as a straightforward news item and may carry more credibility with the readers.

Organisations employing press or public relations officers ensure that good relationships are cultivated with a few key journalists who can be relied upon to listen.

Radio or TV interviews

In other instances, it is the media who initiate contact with the organisation, asking for information or comment. Such approaches can range from an informal telephone call from the local paper asking for immediate comment, to a pre-arranged interview on radio or TV. All such contacts, however informal, need to be handled with care. Calls from journalists need to be handled with extra care, as they may be manipulating what you say in order to flesh out or substantiate their own story.

The essential requirement, when telephoned by a journalist, is to check the status of a conversation before giving any information or making any comment. Be very cautious about saying anything before asking questions such as 'what is the purpose of your call, are you getting background information or is this for the record'?

More time is available to consider what needs to be said in a pre-arranged radio or TV interview. It is usual, before the interview starts, for the interviewer to outline the intended subject matter of his or her questions.

The key to handling such interviews successfully is to decide in advance on the one or two important points to be got across, regardless of what questions are asked. Good interviewees are not passive respondents who allow the interviewer to control the style and scope of the verbal exchange. A media interview is neither a test of the ability to say as little as possible under interrogation nor an occasion to feed the interviewer with the replies that, from a media viewpoint, make good television. It is an opportunity to promote one's case to a wide audience.

The interviewer is, in practice, unlikely to ask the ideal question from the interviewee's standpoint. A short, crisp statement is needed encapsulating the most important point to be made, and think how this can be given in response to whatever question might be asked.

Now read the main points overleaf.

MAIN POINTS FROM CHAPTER NINE

- Negotiations cannot be conducted through the media, but the media can be used to influence the attitudes of those concerned, as well as, where appropriate-public understanding and support.

- The common characteristics of media communications of all kinds are accuracy, clarity and reasonableness.

- Press advertisements offer full control over what is said, but their status as advertisements may reduce their credibility.

- Press releases offer initial control over content, but it cannot be guaranteed that they will be reproduced fully or at all.

- Press releases need to be written in the style of the media to which they are being issued.

- Journalists may be assisted or persuaded to write news stories. These may carry more credibility than company statements, but incur the risk of error or distortion.

- Radio or TV interviews should be seen as opportunities to put across a message in clear, simple terms, regardless of the precise questions to be asked.

10

REFLECTING ON THE PRINCIPLES OF NEGOTIATION

As we have worked our way through this book, we have concentrated on the human elements affecting negotiation and looked at the importance of implementing agreements, along with the importance of understanding what to do if negotiations break down or the agreements not kept to. In addition, we have looked at the role of written and oral communication and the role of the media in the negotiation process.

It is now time to reflect on what we have read.

The main issues

Negotiation is a mixture of science and art, a dynamic interactive process and needs to be conducted in a way that is well planned and yet at the same time flexible. To negotiate successfully you must see the process totally, take a very broad view and continue to do so through the process. This means that you must have a good grasp of the principles involved.

The principles summarised:

- Definition: negotiation is about bargaining to reach a mutually agreeable outcome. This is the win-win concept

- Never neglect preparation. Have a clear plan but remain flexible at all times

- Participants must regard each other as equals. Mutual respect is essential to both the conduct of negotiations and the outcome

- Negotiation is about discussion rather than debate

- Put your cards on the table, at least on major issues

- Patience is very important in negotiations. Delay is better than a poor outcome

- Empathy is important. The need to put yourself in the others shoes is paramount

- State objectives very clearly

- Avoid confrontation. Do not put yourself in a position that you cannot get out of and avoid rows and arguments

- Treat disagreement very carefully

- Deal with concessions progressively. What concessions have to be made, make them unwillingly and one by one

- Be realistic and do not expect perfection

- Use openness but not comprehensively. Declaring your plans may be useful to the discussion. You may want to hide the motivation behind them.

- Set your sights high and settle as high as possible

- Keep up your guard

- Remain professional

- Never underestimate others

- End negotiations on a positive note.

Like any interactive process, negotiation is very dependent on a number of factors. The following are some of those factors:

- Select the right starting point. Your plan should allow for you to take the initiative and quickly get on to your agenda

- Start as high as possible then any trading can move you to a position not far below your starting point

- Never make your feelings that obvious. Negotiations are like a game of poker in that you do not want to allow the other side to see how you are feeling

- Make use of silence

- Keep a look out for early difficulties. Let a mutual rapport build up before you approach difficult issues

- Do not exaggerate facts

- Communicate very clearly. Leave nothing confused or unclear

- Be seen to go with the other persons way of doing things, at least to some degree

- Do not push too hard as this can lead to a situation where both parties are unwilling to give too much

- When you have finished negotiations, stop and conclude the matter. Do not allow further changes to what you have agreed.

There are several elements that must be avoided. Never:

- Over-react if the outcomes of negotiations or responses are negative

- allow yourself to become over emotional. This will weaken your overall resolve

- agree to something that you really do not want.

Negotiation is underpinned by a basic list of techniques that should serve as the structure for discussions. Experience is the most important element. From experience you can learn from mistakes and hopefully never repeat them.

Preparation is the key to successful negotiations. Many people do not prepare and then lose out in the negotiating round. Awareness of the process is equally important. If you are actively aware of the overall process then negotiations will be that much easier.

Confidence is also paramount. Planning is the starting point for confidence in negotiations. If you know what you want, have aimed high in the outset and have a plan through which you can achieve your aims then you will be confident.

Finally, be aware that all agreements reached through negotiation have to be implemented. Knowledge is required of the different remedies available should the process breakdown after agreement.

Good luck.

CASE STUDIES
AND EXERCISE

Case Studies

The three examples outlined overleaf show particular circumstances, each with a varying degree of difficulty. The cases become progressively harder to resolve and each requires varying degrees of skills. The final case is the most difficult of all.

The first case is one where the desired outcomes of both parties are very similar. The second case demonstrates what may happen where the outcomes and the obstacles are greater within a business setting. The third case highlights the difficulties faced where complete intransigence is encountered and involves the construction and planning process.

Case 1.Negotiations in the work place

David works for a medium size advertising company and is seeking promotion to a higher paid job with better prospects. Over the past two years the company has changed shape and David has assumed a lot more responsibility and also has extra managerial responsibilities. He needs to ascertain whether or not his employer will negotiate a new position for him based on his changed job or whether they will decide to recruit outside.

The personnel director, Michael needs to ensure that the post is filled by the right person, someone who is capable. However, he also needs to ensure that money is not wasted.

David knows enough to plan for the meeting. He has considered the following:

• The nature of the new job

• His own strengths and why the company should employ him

• The package he considers appropriate

The package has plenty of variables, such as salary, car, expenses, bonuses, pensions etc.

David considers his approach to the forthcoming negotiations and what impression he will make. Too strong in this particular circumstance and he may be thought too difficult. Too soft and this may convey weakness. Therefore, it is essential that David does the following:

- Prioritize the variables

- Decide on an initial approach that will convey the correct message.

The personnel director has also prepared. He wants to be able to confirm the appointment. He has also thought through all the variables.

Both parties want something good for the company and yet are also initially adversaries. They are, however, equally matched. A win-win outcome is desirable for both. David wants to accept the post without too many regrets about the package. Michael wants him too accept, move into the post and carry on working. Therefore, the goals are not so different.

The way the two parties conduct themselves will affect the outcome. Whatever the outcome, it will not be something that just happened. It will depend on the skills of both and how they each deploy techniques involved in communication generally and negotiation in particular. The two parties will make the outcome what it is.

Case 2. Negotiation in business

This case involves a medium size publishing company, Diamond Publishing limited. Diamond publishing has had a good relationship with its printers for three years, having 90 days credit and a good scale of prices for printed matter.

However, over the last month, the printer has stated that it is changing focus and is moving towards long run journal publishing. Therefore, Diamond publishing's print contract must be terminated.

The managing director of Diamond has made contact with other printers and has negotiated a deal with one, with whom he places an order after having received what seem to be favorable estimates. The estimates are based on the receipt of future work which will make the job economically worthwhile.

The work is duly finished, although it is late. When the invoices arrive for the work, to the managing directors dismay they are 50% higher than the original estimate. The printer explains that the material supplied to them originally was not as specified, more work has gone into production and therefore higher costs incurred. This is the reason for the increase.

The publisher has organized a meeting with the printer to resolve the problem and to set the agenda for the future.

In this situation, the publisher stands to lose a lot of money and a potentially stable printing arrangement with preferential credit terms.

The printer stands to lose further work with the publisher. However, there may be a loss on these first jobs.

In this situation, clearly both parties must:

- Outline the possible advantages and disadvantages of severing the relationship with each other

- The publisher must try to persuade the printer that by lowering the invoice costs, both present and future, more work will come their way

The printer must plan an approach with all the variables clear. Will it try to influence the outcome of discussions by persuading the publisher that it should pay the initial higher price because of the extra work or will it accept a lower initial invoice in the light of future works.

Both parties want a win-win situation but both may wish to adopt an initial stance that is favorable to them in the short term.

There are a number of ways this could go. However, the nature and type of person that each face will be of the utmost importance in the final outcome.

Intransigence may be one possibility. In this case neither party will achieve what they wish. The process of persuasion through reasoning is very important. The laying out of ultimate objectives and the recognizing of variables underpins the negotiating strategy.

Case 3. Negotiation in business-2

This involves a housing association that wishes to develop 40 houses for people in need. The local authority in whose area the association wishes to develop has also received a request from a private builder who wishes to develop housing for sale on the site. The builder has argued that the need for low cost housing is not great and that there are many people with disposable income in the area who could pay for housing on the open market.

The local authority planners have considered the merits of each proposal and have decided that it is not so supportive of the housing associations plans. However, the association is desperate to develop in the area and is convinced that there is a need to be fulfilled, both in new housing and also to create extra mobility.

The private house builder has concrete proposals for development and for the likely take up of private houses and flats. The planners see that a private development will be favored by the local people who have a negative view of "problem tenants".

There are, therefore, three parties to the negotiations that will ensue. The local authority, the private house builder and the housing association. The housing association has the hardest job of all, trying to persuade the local authority of the merits of allowing it to go ahead and develop and also trying to overturn the objections of the private house builder, even perhaps persuading them to enter into a joint partnership.

The strategy in this sort of negotiation, which is not a win-win situation but very much a situation which is stacked initially against the housing association, is for the association to have identified all of the variables, such as housing need, mobility options, and increased housing for those on lower income and also to have clearly identified its ultimate aims in the light of those variables.

A plan is needed, which involves changing the culture of the initial negotiations so that those in power, and those whose plan is favored, are brought round to the way of thinking of the association. This will be achieved by clearly communicating the views of the association.

The private house builder will, initially, probably be intransigent and will need to be persuaded of the associations case before considering possible proposals for a mixed development. However, in the first instance, profit will be the motive and the developers concern to maintain the status of the scheme so that potential buyers are not put off.

Both will be leveling their needs wants and desires towards the planners who hold power.

In order to gain something from the negotiations, the housing association has to clearly map out its strategy. All of the relevant variables have to be identified and prioritized. The association has to aim as high as possible but must be prepared to compromise, if the chance arises, and enter into a mixed development.

A lot rests on the attitudes of the planners and the private house builder. However, the association has the difficult job of persuading both parties that it should either be allowed to develop or to join forces with the private developer.

Clear communication of identified advantages, all advantages, is paramount. The association will gain nothing through the negotiations if the other side is not clear about the need or the advantages of participation. The need to be flexible is clear along with enhanced powers of persuasion.

Planning is the crucial element. This will give confidence and will enable the association to doggedly pursue its aims and not to crumble in the face of intransigence.

Exercise.

On the basis of the third case study outlined above put yourself in the place of the housing association and define your own aims and objectives putting together a strategy that will enable you to achieve your goal.

Glossary of terms

Concessions Those aspects of any deal that must be arranged and agreed during the process of negotiation.

Empathy: The ability to put yourself in another persons place and to understand their point of view.

Objectives: Desired results. They need to be specific and measurable and linked to a timeframe.

Power: Factors, tangible or otherwise, that give one person an edge.

Stance: The position taken up by a negotiator at any particular stage or over any particular issue.

Strategy: A course of action designed to achieve specific objectives.

Trading: The process of arranging, and sometimes exchanging, concessions. This is an inherent element of the negotiation process.

Variables: The raw materials of trading. The elements of what you have and what you need.

Win-Win: A common way of referring to a satisfactory outcome for both parties.

Index